Dan

The Angel Who Wore Shoes

Illustrated by
Maureen Carter

Series editor: Rod Nesbitt

Heinemann International Literature and Textbooks
A division of Heinemann Educational Books Ltd
Halley Court, Jordan Hill, Oxford OX2 8EJ

Heinemann Educational Boleswa
PO Box 10103, Village Post Office, Gaborone, Botswana
Heinemann Educational Books (Nigeria) Ltd
PMB 5205, Ibadan

LONDON EDINBURGH PARIS MADRID
ATHENS BOLOGNA MELBOURNE
SYDNEY AUCKLAND PORTSMOUTH (NH)
SINGAPORE TOKYO

© Dan Fulani 1993
First published by Heinemann International Literature
and Textbooks in 1993

British Library Cataloguing in Publication Data
A catalogue record for this book is available
from the British Library

ISBN 0 435 89172 3

The right of Dan Fulani to be identified as
the author of this work has been asserted by him in accordance
with the Copyright, Designs and Patents Act 1988.

Glossary
Difficult words are listed alphabetically on page 29

Printed and bound in Great Britain by
George Over Limited, Rugby and London
93 94 95 96 10 9 8 7 6 5 4 3 2 1

Tanko liked to eat pumpkins. He grew them beside his house. As they grew, they climbed over the roof of the house. But Tanko was a lazy farmer. He was too lazy to give the pumpkins any water. The dry season came and it stopped raining. Very soon the pumpkins died. Tanko looked at his dead crop and was very sad.

'If you watered your pumpkins, they wouldn't die,' said his neighbour Gumi.

Tanko didn't say anything. He looked at Gumi's house. He could see Gumi's pumpkins growing over the thatched roof. They were big, juicy pumpkins and they were ready to eat. Gumi was a very good farmer. He worked hard on his farm. He always watered his pumpkins in the dry season.

Gumi was a good farmer but he was not very clever. Tanko was a bad farmer but he was clever. Tanko was as clever as a hyena. A hyena steals its food. It steals the food after another animal has killed it. Tanko looked at Gumi's pumpkins for a long time. They looked so good that he could almost taste them. Tanko had to have one of those pumpkins.

Tanko thought and thought about Gumi's pumpkins. Then he had an idea. He would steal one of the pumpkins. He started to count them. He counted seventeen. Gumi would not miss one pumpkin because he had so many. He knew that Gumi wasn't clever. Gumi would not remember how many pumpkins he had growing on his roof. Tanko was certain Gumi would not miss just one pumpkin.

Tanko waited for a very dark night. There were clouds in the sky and the moon was not shining. Tanko crept up to Gumi's house and started to climb on to the roof.

Gumi was a good farmer but he wasn't a good builder. The thatch on the roof of his house was old. He hadn't repaired it for three years. When Tanko climbed on to the roof it started to break.

Tanko tried to jump down but it was too late. The roof broke and Tanko fell into Gumi's house.

Gumi and his wife, Adiza, were asleep in bed. They heard the crash and woke up. They were very frightened and they screamed loudly. Tanko had fallen through the roof and was lying on their bed.

'Help! Help!' they shouted in fear. They could see the dark figure at the bottom of the bed.

It was very dark in the house. The village where they lived was deep in the bush. It was hundreds of kilometres from the nearest town and it had no electricity. Gumi started to search for the kerosene lamp and the matches. But he was so frightened he could not light the match.

Tanko was not hurt. He had fallen on Gumi and Adiza's bed. But how was he going to escape?

Suddenly he thought of a clever plan. He pretended he was an angel.

'God bless you and your wife,' he said. He spoke in a very deep voice because he did not want Gumi to recognise him. 'I am an angel sent from God. Shut your eyes very tightly. If you look at me you will go blind.'

He did not want Gumi to light the lamp and see his face.

Gumi and Adiza shut their eyes. They hid their faces in their pillows.

'God has sent me here,' Tanko said. 'He wants me to take you to Him.'

Gumi and Adiza cried out in fear.

'Oh, help us,' Gumi said. 'Please, help us.'

'Oh, please,' Adiza cried. 'We are still young and our children are only babies. What will they do without us?'

They began to pray to God to save them.

Tanko did not say anything for a moment. Then he spoke very slowly.

'I will ask God to let you live,' he said in his deep voice, 'if you give me all the money in the house.'

'Does God need money?' Gumi asked.

'Yes, of course,' replied Tanko. 'He has to pay for all the things His angels give to people.'

'I hadn't thought of that,' said Gumi.

Tanko was carrying a bag. He was going to put the pumpkin in it. Now he gave the bag to Gumi.

'I want you to put all your money in this bag,' he said. 'When I say "begin", you can open your eyes. Then you must collect all your money. If you do not put all your money in the bag, I will take you to God.'

Tanko hid under the bed. Then he shouted, 'Begin.'

Gumi and Adiza ran to find all their money. Gumi had hidden some notes under a stone near the door. Adiza had some coins tied up in a piece of cloth. Then she remembered she had some more coins in a pot in the kitchen. Gumi took all the money he had in his trouser pockets. They put all the money in Tanko's bag.

Tanko told them to close their eyes again. Then he crawled out from under the bed. He took the bag and ran to the door.

'God has let you live,' he shouted. 'Get down on your knees. Thank Him for His kindness.'

Tanko ran out of the house. Gumi and Adiza knelt beside the bed and thanked God. They were very happy to be alive.

The next morning Gumi told his good friend Sumo about the angel.

'A terrible thing happened last night,' he said. He was very excited. 'It was in the middle of the night. Adiza and I were fast asleep. Suddenly there was a crash and we woke up. There at the bottom of the bed was an angel. He told us he had come to take us to God.

'We both begged the angel to help us,' Gumi went on. 'He said he would let us live if we gave him all our money. When we gave him the money he went away.'

Sumo was very wise. He didn't believe that angels took money from people.

'I don't believe it,' he said. 'I would like to see the hole in your roof. He must have been a very heavy angel.'

Sumo walked over to Gumi's house. He looked at the hole in the roof. Then he looked at the sand beside the house. He found a footprint in the sand and he knelt down to look at it very carefully. Sumo stood up and began to laugh. He laughed until tears came into his eyes. The tears ran down his cheeks. He laughed and laughed and laughed. He laughed so much he had to sit down.

When Sumo stopped laughing, he looked at Gumi.

'This is a very strange angel,' he said. 'He came to your house without any wings.'

'What do you mean?' asked Gumi. 'I don't understand.'

'Look at these footprints,' replied Sumo. 'This angel wears shoes. He wears shoes made from old car tyres. I don't think an angel visited you last night. I think it was just an ordinary thief.'

Gumi looked at the marks in the sand. He looked at one footprint and then another one.

'You're right,' he said. 'These marks are from an old tyre. The thief is someone who cut up an old tyre to make a pair of shoes. But what can we do? A lot of the villagers cut up old tyres to make shoes.'

Sumo smiled and pointed at the footprints.

'Look very hard,' he said. 'Look at that footprint there.' He pointed at one of the footprints in the sand. 'Can you see the letters DU? We must look for someone who has the letters DU on his right shoe. If we can find the shoe we will find the thief.'

Sumo started to laugh again.

'We might even catch an angel,' he said. 'Maybe angels without wings wear shoes made from old tyres.'

19

Gumi and Sumo went to the chief of the village. Gumi told the chief what had happened to him and Adiza. He told him about hearing a crash. He told him about the angel who asked for money.

The chief listened very carefully. Then he walked to Gumi's house. He looked at the hole in the roof. He looked at the bed under the hole. He looked at the footprints in the sand.

When he saw the letters DU in the dust, he began to smile.

'I know what to do,' he said. 'We will call all the men in the village to a meeting. Then we will ask them to walk on the sand in front of us. We will soon find the angel who wears shoes.'

The chief sent his three sons to tell the villagers to come to his house.

The villagers soon began to arrive in front of the chief's house. A family came, and then two more. Some women arrived from the fields. The children ran about playing and shouting. Tanko was one of the last to come.

The chief sat in a chair. He told his sons to sweep the sand clean in front of him. Then he spoke to the villagers in a loud voice.

'This is a simple test,' he said. 'I want the men to walk on the sand in front of me.' He pointed at the ground.

One by one the villagers walked in front of the chief. After each villager had walked over the sand, the chief looked at the footprints. Then the chief told his sons to sweep the sand again. One by one the men of the village walked across the sand.

At last it was Tanko's turn to walk across the sand. When Tanko reached the other side, he looked at the chief. But the chief was looking at the footprints. He immediately saw the letters DU in the sand. He knew that Tanko was the thief.

'Last night,' he told the villagers, 'an angel fell through Gumi's roof. But he was an angel without any wings. This angel stole all Gumi's money.'

'I don't understand,' said Tanko nervously. 'What has this to do with me?'

'You are the angel who had no wings,' replied the chief. 'Look at your footprints. Do you see the letters DU? We found the same footprints outside Gumi's house. You aren't an angel. You are the thief who stole Gumi's money. The police will want to know why your footprints were outside Gumi's house.'

The police station was five kilometres away. The chief told his eldest son to get his bicycle.

'I want you to ride to the police station,' the chief said. 'Tell the police that we have caught a thief. A thief who pretended to be an angel.'

The chief's son rode as fast as he could. When the police heard about the robbery, they came at once.

They searched Tanko's house. They found the money which Tanko had stolen in a box. It was still in the pumpkin bag. The police arrested Tanko. They tied his hands together behind his back.

'I think they should tie his wings together too,' laughed Sumo. 'We don't want him to fly away.'

Tanko didn't eat pumpkin for a long time. They don't give you pumpkin to eat when you are in prison.

Questions

1 What animal does the author say Tanko is like? Why does he say this?
2 What does Tanko tell Gumi and his wife to do so that they won't see him?
3 What does he do to change his voice?
4 Gumi and Adiza look for money in four different places. Where do they look?
5 Why does Sumo say the angel must have been very heavy?
6 How do Sumo and Gumi know that it was not an angel at all?
7 How does the chief plan to trap the thief?

Activities

1 Draw a picture of Tanko falling through the roof of Gumi's house.
2 Ask your teacher if you can go outside and make footprints in the dust. Make drawings of all the different footprints. When you go back into class, you can play a game. Try to remember who made the footprints.

Glossary

crash (page 6) loud noise of something breaking

footprints (page 16) the marks made by feet or shoes in the dust

notes (page 12) paper money

ordinary (page 17) not special, just a thief not an angel

pretended (page 8) made believe he was an angel

The Junior African Writers Series is designed to provide interesting and varied African stories both for pleasure and for study. There are five graded levels in the series.

Level 2 is suited to readers who have been studying English for four to five years. The content and language have been carefully controlled to increase fluency in reading.

Content The plots are simple and the number of characters is kept to a minimum. The information is presented in small, manageable amounts and the illustrations reinforce the text.

Language Reading is a learning experience, and although the choice of words is carefully controlled, new words, important to the story, are also introduced. These are contextualised, recycled through the story and explained in the glossary. They also appear in other stories at Level 2.

Glossary Difficult words which learners may not know and which are not made clear in the illustrations have been listed alphabetically at the back of the book. The definitions refer to the way the word is used in the story and the page reference is for the word's first use.

Questions and Activities The questions give useful comprehension practice and ensure that the reader has followed and understood the story. The activities develop themes and ideas introduced and can be done as pairwork or groupwork in class, or as homework.

Resource material Further resources are being developed to assist in the teaching of reading with Jaws titles.

Other Jaws titles at Level 2

The Picture that Came Alive, Hugh Lewin, 0 435 89167 7

The Buried Treasure, Akachi Adimora-Ezeigbo, 0 435 89169 3

The Ghost of Ratemo, James Ngumy, 0 435 89171 5

Kagiso's Mad Uncle, Keith Whiteley, 0 435 89164 2

The Magic Pool, Gaele Mogwe, 0 435 89166 9